Precia,

"You are a blessing to others"
1 Peter 4:8
Col. 3:12

Love
Vikki

RECOGNIZING THE

FRUIT OF THE SPIRIT

IN YOU

VIKKI HARRIS

Recognizing the Fruit of the Spirit

ISBN: 978-1492366393

Copyright© 2014 Vikki Harris

Highest Praise Management
a.k.a. Plant A Seed Ministries

Unless otherwise identified, Scripture quotations are from the New International Version of the Bible.

The New Merriam-Webster Dictionary, based on Webster's Third New International Dictionary, Unabridged is used as reference for portions of the definitions of love, joy, peace, longsuffering, gentleness, goodness, faith, meekness and temperance.

Contact Author: (617) 433-7729
Website: www.vikkiharris.com
Email: contactme@vikkiharris.com
Facebook: www.facebook.com/authorvikkiharris

ACKNOWLEDGEMENTS

Message to my Son,
Christopher Harris
If you utilize the wisdom God gives you
in every endeavor you undertake
and apply the principles of the
Fruit of the Spirit,
success, love, peace and joy will be yours.
Love Always, Mom

Special Thanks To:
Cheryl Carey
Charlotte Harris
Karen Sumpter-Sanders
Elaine Thomas
Rene Weathers

Contents

Introduction

Psalm 51:5 reads "Surely I was sinful at birth, sinful from the time my mother conceived me." After reading this scripture I began to wonder if this is why some of my positive attempts to help others have been misconstrued as self righteous behavior, a disingenuous action or taken advantage of as if motivated by weakness. I am sure we all agree that we all have a sinful nature and, at times, do not need reasons or provocation to exhibit negative behavior. But I wonder if it is our sinful nature that causes us to view good deeds as negative? When our lens is tainted because of our own personal trials and tribulations of life, do we view others actions, situations or circumstances fairly?

As the world is now, we are given many opportunities and can find many excuses to consciously commit sins against others on a daily basis. I believe that our treatment of others would be different if our bodies were riddled with holes for everyone to see the amount of pain and turmoil we hide inside. Regardless of our feelings or thoughts, we are suppose to refrain from doing wrong and seek after God's goodness. In order to completely find a deeper meaning, I had to realize that God's goodness was not just defined as what He does for me, but is defined as it relates to His virtues – the content of His character. As I began thinking on how I can change the way I am perceived by others and ensure my words, deeds and thoughts are not influenced solely by my own understanding, I had to figure out what part of the Bible best described God's characteristics that I could emulate. For me, it was best described in the fruit of the spirit. In order for me to learn more about the fruit of the spirit, I had to evaluate the meaning of each fruit.

The fruit of the spirit is considered one fruit collectively with nine parts. It is described in Galatians 5:22-23 **"But the fruit of the Spirit is love, joy, peace, longsuffering, gentleness, goodness, faith, meekness, temperance: against such things there is no law."** I believe that each fruit is worked into the Christian human spirit as we grow older and teaches us about God's divine personality and character traits. Simply saying that in one's lifetime there are experiences that introduce, teach and/or cultivate each individual fruit which help us to curb our fleshly behavior and adopt a more Christ like attitude.

In writing this book, my first challenge was to be truthful with myself and evaluate my character flaws and what I know about the meaning of each individual fruit. This was a tedious process because I had to learn the true definition of each fruit, and then identify each incident and/or circumstance I believe was used to teach me about love, joy, peace, longsuffering, gentleness, goodness, faith, meekness and temperance. In doing so, I was able to identify my own personal growth as patience, wisdom, humility, compassion, forgiveness, empathy, trust, and perseverance... as more of God's spirit was illuminated in me. This was a challenge for me to identify and write, however I believe I have been successful in doing so.

Each fruit is explained by actual situations or circumstances that have happened to me. In some instances, I changed the names or obliterated a name to protect the person's identity because I want the focus to remain on the subject matter and not the person as you read. The people portrayed were only an instrument used for my personal growth and development and this book was not written to solely portray them as having bad character. Furthermore, I encourage you to not focus solely on people and their interactions in your own life without considering the purpose of each encounter. Lastly, I am not trying to portray myself as a person that always has the best answer or response because these stories are recited as the individual fruit was being cultivated unbeknownst to me.

Can you identify the fruit of the spirit in your life? When did you learn the true meaning of each fruit: love, joy, peace, longsuffering, gentleness, goodness, faith, meekness and temperance? What was the defining moment or moments you knew, that you knew? In this writing I am sharing my personal experiences that helped me identify the fruit of the spirit in me and praying that as you read, you are able to relate, identify or discover each one in you.

Love
(strong affection, warm attachment, to feel a passion, devotion, or tenderness...)

It was almost 2:00 a.m. on Thursday, December 23, 1994 when my mother shook me awake from my sleep and said "Vikki, I need your help". As I looked at her, I thought, "This is a dream. No, this is real." I immediately leaped from my bed and followed her into her bedroom.

I recall it was the week of Christmas, and, in my opinion, it was going to be a very good week. I was exceptionally happy because on Monday I had moved into a newly updated apartment not far from my parent's home. I could not sleep in my new apartment right away because I had to work the remainder of the week and did not have an opportunity to clean, unpack or assemble the beds until the upcoming weekend. I anticipated the joy I would have living in my new apartment, but I was happy to stay at my parent's home throughout the week. Besides, it was my father's favorite holiday and Christmas was always a festive time of year at their home.

During the week, every morning when I awoke I heard my father say to my son, "When you turn 3, I am going to put you in karate classes. When you turn 4, I am going to take you to another barber to get your hair cut. I do not like the way your mother has it cut and when you turn 5....." Each morning I chuckled as I lay in bed listening because he repeated the same thing as they ate breakfast together.

I quickly recognized a pattern forming. In the morning my father fixed breakfast for my son and conversed with him while they ate. Every night around 1:00 a.m. my father woke up complaining of heartburn and indigestion. Well in fairness I should say this happened Monday and Tuesday night. I was still awake both nights and asked if he wanted tea or something to settle the heartburn. He simply replied, "No, I will drink some warm water and go back to bed. Thanks. Goodnight." He then proceeded to go to the bathroom and back to bed.

On Wednesday night, early Thursday morning between 1:00 and 2:00 a.m. I heard my father wake up, walk down the hallway burping (as I had grown accustomed to hearing), turn on the water in the kitchen, flush the toilet in the bathroom and then return to bed. This particular morning I did not see him because I was in my bedroom, however I heard his movements and realized he had heartburn/indigestion again.

However, this was not simply heartburn/indigestion. When my mother woke me needing my assistance it was because my father was having a heart attack as he slept and she wanted me to call an ambulance.

As we awaited the arrival of the ambulance my mother frantically called my father's name attempting to wake him. She also tried to sit him up because the sound he was making led us to believe he may have been choking. We did not realize that sound is typically referred to as the "death rattle". I asked my mother what was happening and she answered, "He is dying". As I looked in her eyes I knew she was correct. That is the moment that I lost it! It was unimaginable that my father was dying. I thought I was still dreaming and this couldn't happen to my father at that moment. When the ambulance and fire truck arrived, they attempted to reset his heart by using a defibrillator. They explained that there was a faint heartbeat, they needed to transport him to the hospital and my mother, son and I should follow the ambulance.

Shortly after our arrival, we were escorted to a private room "for our comfort" as the hospital typically states when preparing to deliver bad news to a family. A physician soon entered and explained they attempted to resuscitate my father, but my dad had passed on.

I was devastated. How can a body just stop breathing? How can God possibly love me if He allowed my Dad to die? How can the only person that loved me unconditionally leave me? I had many questions and no answers. All I felt was pain and numbness if there is a way to feel both at the same time – I felt it. I kept thinking, "Now what do I do? How could this happen? This is a nightmare."

Prior to that night, I never thought about love or its meaning because it was around me all the time. I was loved dearly. My Dad loved me no matter what I did and I knew it. His love was unconditional and the older I became, the more I realized how special it was. I was

Daddy's girl so I did not think I needed to know anything more about love.

However, once my father died I became acutely aware of the lack of unconditional love in my life. I began to wonder how or if I would ever have someone love me like that again. I compared every friendship, kinship and relationship to the kind of love I had always known. Upon examination, each one would disappoint me in one way or another. Could there really be a love better than the love I shared with my Dad? I did not think so.

Little did I know my Dad's death was not the end of love as I had known it, but it was my introduction to unconditional love for a lifetime. I had taken love for granted and not really thought about what it was or how it should be freely given until I no longer thought it was unconditionally given to me. I knew my entire family loved me, but in my opinion, their love was not unconditional (of course that was not completely true, but it was how I thought/felt during my time of grieving.)

From 1994 to early 1999 I was on a quest to get answers to my questions. I began occasionally reading the

Bible and asking questions. In 1999 I found scriptures in 1 Corinthians 13:1-3 which read **"If I speak in the tongues of men or of angels, but do not have love, I am only a resounding gong or a clanging cymbal. If I have the gift of prophecy and can fathom all mysteries and all knowledge, and if I have a faith that can move mountains, but do not have love, I am nothing. If I give all I possess to the poor and give over my body to hardship that I may boast, but do not have love, I gain nothing."** There it is that's how I felt....I had nothing because there was a hole in me and something was missing. I immediately knew I needed to find out if the Bible had more answers to what I was lacking so automatically, I began to read more.

Since the time of my father's death I had not attended church regularly. Actually, there were periods of time that I did not go to church at all. However the more I read the Bible the more I realized that there was so much more to learn. I realized I had to read the Bible and go to church to get the best understanding from the scriptures. So, I read more, learned more, attended church and began to understand more about the love of God. I finally made a decision to be reinstated at the church I had attended when

I was younger. As part of the reinstatement process I had to select a "life verse" from the Bible. This was challenging for me because I had experienced suffering, tragedies, and traveled down many paths (many that I did not need to venture down) and one verse could not sum it all up for me.

In preparation for reinstatement, I diligently read and studied the word of God. I eventually was led to select three verses - Romans 5:3-5 – "**Not only so, but we also glory in our sufferings, because we know that suffering produces perseverance; perseverance, character; and character, hope. And hope does not put us to shame, because God's love has been poured out into our hearts through the Holy Spirit, who has been given to us.**" This explained my past, present and future. It also gave me hope for the love I was searching for - God's love.

On the night I was reinstated I prepared and read the following to the congregation: "To surrender all and accept Jesus as my Lord and Savior has been the best decision I have made in years. Thanks to my family members, close friends and prayer life I have learned to be thankful for all things. Furthermore, I have learned that it is His will that matters – not mine." After confessing this I felt a release in my spirit like never before. I keep this note on my desk today as a reminder of the night I recommitted my life to Christ.

My grieving process lasted 5 years before I realized my Dad was in a better place. I finally became thankful because he was not in pain, not suffering and there was no more sorrow. I stopped focusing on my desires and began to think of my Dad and what his life would have been like if he had been resuscitated. Even though he did not appear ill outwardly, his heart was badly damaged. More than likely he would have been unable to care for himself and his basic needs if he had survived the heart attack. I finally realized he would have been miserable and if I truly loved my Dad, I had to realize what was best for him.

Opening up and learning more about God (my heavenly father) and releasing my desire to physically see and interact with my Dad (my earthly father) alive, I learned more about love as stated in 1 Corinthians 13:4- 8 – **"Love is patient, love is kind. It does not envy, it does not boast, it is not proud. It does not dishonor others, it is not self-seeking, it is not easily angered, it keeps no record of wrongs. Love does not delight in evil but**

rejoices with the truth. It always protects, always trusts, always hopes, always perseveres. Love never fails." I did not have an understanding of love prior to losing my father, but once I began researching, I found all the answers in the Bible. I discovered the love of my heavenly father was also unconditional and no matter what I did, He still loved me and His love is eternal.

I still wish I could see, talk to and laugh with my Dad, but I thank God, He used my Dad's way of loving me unconditionally to teach me the most important lesson in my life – all about love – God's love.

What is your definition of love? Do you know the difference between being loved and being loved unconditionally? Do you know that God loves you unconditionally (agape love, God's love)?

Now that I have shared how I discovered the meaning of love, I want to share more of what the Bible states about it. In 1 Timothy 1:12-16 Paul who is an Apostle of God (representative of God) explains that he was once a persecutor of Christians which made him one of the worse sinners. Yet, God loved him (and us) so much that He sent His son, Jesus the Christ, to the world to save sinners like Paul (you and I). He (we) received God's grace and mercy - God's love – even though he was a blasphemer, persecutor and violent man. God's love supersedes anything we can do to earn it. 1 Timothy 1:12-16 reads, "**I thank Christ Jesus our Lord, who has given me strength, that he considered me trustworthy, appointing me to his service. Even though I was once a blasphemer and a persecutor and a violent man, I was shown mercy because I acted in ignorance and unbelief. The grace of our Lord was poured out on me abundantly, along with the faith and love that are in Christ Jesus. Here is a trustworthy saying that deserves full acceptance: Christ Jesus came into the world to save sinners—of whom I am the worst. But for that very reason I was shown mercy so that in me, the worst of sinners, Christ Jesus might display his immense patience as an example for those who would believe in him and receive eternal life.**"

This scripture is not implying that we can do whatever we want. Read it again. "**I was shown mercy because I acted in ignorance and unbelief.**" Once we are saved (confess with our mouth and believe in our heart that

Jesus was raised from the dead, read Romans 10:9), there are certain behaviors, responses and actions that we should no longer allow ourselves to exhibit. Jesus came as the sacrifice for our past, present and future sins by dying on the cross because God loved us that much.

God does not merely love; He is love. Everything God does flows from His unconditional love for us and He is always with us.

Above all, love each other deeply,
because love covers over a multitude
of sins.

1 Peter 4:8

Love - understanding no matter the love your
parents, husband and Kids have for you.
The love of good is so much greater.

Joy

(a feeling of happiness that comes from success, good fortune, or a sense of well being...)

I learned the true meaning of joy in what I believe is an unusual way in 2001 when my sister, Cheryl, had a total knee replacement. After her knee replacement surgery she had rehabilitation, knee manipulation exercises and therapy as planned by her physician. But, by the third week Cheryl was experiencing pain much worse than prior to the surgery. She no longer had full range of motion and could not bend her knee more than 20%. This outcome was disheartening. The purpose of the surgery was to allow her to have pain free full range of motion when moving, standing, sitting and/or bending her knee.

Cheryl soon discovered her knee surgery was unsuccessful. The surgery was a total failure and left her in excruciating pain 24 hours per day. Her leg remained swollen from extreme inflammation and the pain became unbearable. Prior to the surgery she had pain in her knee, but she did not have excruciating pain all the time. Also prior to surgery, she could bend her knee.

After 6-8 months of agonizing pain and intensive rehabilitation, she decided to get a second opinion. After examination, the new physician realized that too much scar tissue had formed under the new knee cap and around the bone for her knee to bend properly. He proposed removing her knee cap again, scraping the scar tissue and replacing it with another new knee. When I heard that she was going to have the surgery redone I researched the process of knee replacement and I learned that the operation consists of replacing a knee joint with a man-made (artificial) joint. The artificial joint is called prosthesis. The prosthesis is secured by welding it to the bone. I could not imagine the amount of pain she had experienced and now they were going to remove the first welded prosthesis and weld another one to her bone. This was unimaginable, but as long as it worked, it was going to be worth it.

The second physician truly believed he could clean up the scar tissue which he thought caused most of the problem. Unfortunately, there was far more scar tissue than what he had anticipated. The second knee replacement did not improve her condition and perhaps made it worse. To this day Cheryl is still unable to bend her leg and has chronic pain.

One day while conversing with her on the phone she said "hold on, I have to scratch my foot." I laughed and teased her because I thought she was being a bit dramatic. I laughed and asked, "Why do I have to hold on for you to scratch your foot?" She simply answered, "Because I can not scratch my foot." I continued to laugh with no real thought about her response or condition.

Two days later I was sitting in a chair and my foot began to itch. As I bent over to scratch it, I thought about the movements I made to scratch my foot. The light bulb in my head burned bright. I had to bend my leg to easily scratch my foot and I was able to scratch because my leg was able to bend. That realization overwhelmed me to tears. Unlike Cheryl whose leg no longer bends, mine does. At that moment I realized that God allowed me to bend my leg to complete a taken for granted task such as scratching my foot. He did not have to, but He did. That is when I understood the true definition of joy.

Prior to this, my understanding of joy was defined as what I felt when I spent time with friends and had fun for the moment. Now I understand that is simply considered fun or pleasure. Joy is an unspeakable deep down feeling of gratitude for something you know you did not earn, but are blessed to have. I began to understand the joy in waking up in the morning, blinking my eyes, walking down the stairs, using my hands to type, lifting my arms over my head or simply knowing that I have five functioning senses. Wow, I found joy in having the use of my limbs! My eyes were opened to so many things in my life that I was taking for granted. The meaning of Psalm 28:7 became clear which reads "**The Lord is my strength and my shield; my heart trusts in him, and he helps me. My heart leaps for joy, and with my song I praise him.**"

God used my sister's inability to move her leg to teach me the true meaning of joy. I am convinced that God will teach us lessons by using any and everything He has created here on earth.

Smiling outwardly and saying all the right things, as so many of us do, does not bring joy. Joy is looking at the pain (hurt, mean people, fallen world) and smiling because the ray of light that shines through the darkness is Jesus.

Joy is not a tangible gift because we can not see or touch it. It is something we feel in our soul. It is given to us freely and we can recognize it most when we become cognizant and thankful for all things we know we could not provide for ourselves. What I am trying to say is best explained in 1 Corinthians 2:13, **"What we have received is not the spirit of the world, but the Spirit who is from God, so that we may understand what God has freely given us.** What is better than receiving a gift from God?

As for my sister, she does not have a "why me?" in her spirit. She actually appears to be happier than she was prior to her debilitating condition. I think it is because she knows that God continually pours out His love and holds her in the palm of His hand. She knows how blessed she is because God provides all that she needs. Can you recall when you learned what the true meaning of joy is?

The world did not bring this joy

to me and the world

can not

take it away.

Joy - understanding no matter what situation
your in, joy of God will carry you through

Peace
(a state of calm and quiet, freedom from disturbing thoughts or emotions...)

Searching my memory to discover when I consciously began to seek the meaning of peace, I believe it was in 2006 during bible study at a local church. On Monday night the Sunday School Teachers held bible study and invited me to participate because I was a teacher at another local church that did not offer bible study.

While attending the bible study, I learned that the Beatitudes are a set of values that Christ cares about. As Jesus sat on a mountainside he began to teach these values. Matthew 5:3-12 - **"He said: "Blessed are the poor in spirit, for theirs is the kingdom of heaven. Blessed are those who mourn, for they will be comforted. Blessed are the meek, for they will inherit the earth. Blessed are those who hunger and thirst for righteousness, for they will be filled. Blessed are the merciful, for they will be shown mercy. Blessed are the pure in heart, for they will see God. Blessed are the peacemakers, for they will be called children of God. Blessed are those who are persecuted because of righteousness, for theirs is the**

kingdom of heaven. Blessed are you when people insult you, persecute you and falsely say all kinds of evil against you because of me. Rejoice and be glad, because great is your reward in heaven, for in the same way they persecuted the prophets who were before you."

This taught me to understand that Jesus required me to endure all things for His sake. Knowing that Jesus was persecuted; I still did not understand why I thought I was exempt from trials, tribulations and turmoil? During this period of life I understood each scripture literally without pondering previous scriptures, existing culture or any of the considerations I now use to determine the intended translation of a scripture. Therefore, I went through a check list of the Beatitudes to see if I possessed any of the values required of me. I quickly realized my strengths and areas that required great improvement. The area of becoming a peacemaker needed the most work.

I realized that I was the peacemaker if there was a dispute that existed between others because my level of discernment enabled me to help others find common ground and balance. But if the dispute or disagreement was between another person and me, I did not agree with anything other than my point of view. I did not realize that saying what I thought, most often, created a more volatile outcome regardless of whether my statements were truthful or not. I had to learn that peace was more important than my point of view. That was a challenging lesson however I wanted to be blessed and called a child of God.

One of my most recent examples of implementing my desire to maintain peace above all occurred during a trip to my local pharmacy.

As I drove toward the exit of Walgreens parking lot there was a girl walking very slowly in the middle of the parking lot blocking the passage of cars on both sides. I slowed down, waited and then attempted to pass on the right side of the parking lot. I beeped my horn to alert her of my presence as I attempted to pass. She moved slightly to the left without allowing much room for my passage. I inched past her and noticed she appeared distraught, lost in thought and totally unaware of her surroundings.

I stopped driving, lowered my window and waited for her to walk closer to my vehicle so I could ask her if she was okay or needed assistance. As she approached my car she walked closer to the right side of the parking lot further away from where my window was lowered. I thought she was avoiding me, but I did not know if it was intentional. So, I rolled down my right passenger window and leaned toward its opening as she approached.

When she was close enough I asked, "Are you okay?" She responded, "Are you?" with many more expletives than I care to mention. As she yelled and berated me with expletives, she walked faster out of the parking lot and onto the sidewalk in the opposite direction. I did not respond. I waited for traffic to allow me to enter on the main road, drove past her one block, turned into the next parking lot and waited for her to approach.

I was determined to explain what my intentions were. I decided I was not going to allow her to go through her day or life thinking, some lady attempted to fight with, assault or offend her in any way. I was concerned and I wanted her to know the truth.

As she approached I exited my car and greeted her by saying "Hello, I apologize if I startled you, however I wanted to know if you were okay and if there was something I could assist you with?" She looked at me and stated, "Assist me? How could you possibly assist me? My children were just removed from my home, my boyfriend was arrested, I am probably going to get evicted from my apartment and I just had a miscarriage. How can you help me?" Tears were streaming down her face. I replied, "Right now, I can pray with you, refer you to local agencies that can help you and give you a ride to where you are going because your bags look extremely heavy." I further explained to her that I was concerned for her well being.

I do not normally offer a stranger a ride however I was willing to drive her to her destination. I listened to her, prayed with her, gave her information of local organizations that could help her and gave her my phone number in case she wanted to converse more in the future. She apologized for her verbal assault earlier and was extremely happy that I decided to stop and make sure she understood I was trying to help her and not harm her. I had not realized that I startled her when I stopped my vehicle in the parking lot and lowered my window to wait for her. She was defensive because she thought I was waiting to verbally assault her or something worse. I learned a valuable lesson that day and developed a new friendship. We are currently still in contact with one another.

On many occasions I have held my tongue when I was misunderstood and did not attempt to correct or explain my true intent. On this particular day, if I had not pursued her I would have spent the greater part of the day sulking because of the venomous words she screamed at me. I also would have regretted not clarifying my intent. Psalm 34:14 (NIV) states **"Turn from evil and do good; seek peace and pursue it."** Even though I had to humble myself and not speak to her the way she was speaking to me, this encounter proved seeking peace was much more rewarding. I experienced a peace I had never experienced before after pushing past my comfort zone, to pursue and converse with her. I allowed the Lord to guide me, without fear and exposed my heart to a stranger.

There are times when being silent causes more chaos than speaking up and correcting misunderstandings. How often do you remain silent when speaking up could help free you or someone else from bondage, depression or a downtrodden state of mind?

When was the last time you spoke up to ensure someone else had a peaceful experience?

The Lord's peace is given to us when we accept Him as our Lord and Savior. However, we do not seem to accept His peace easily because we still worry and stress over worldly issues. The Lord's peace is not only the absence of arguing or negative situations it is when we turn our will and worry over to God and allow Him to direct our path. When we experience God as Jehovah Shalom we will rest in Him and believe His promises without impatience. Remember Philippians 4:6-7 teaches, "**Do not be anxious about anything, but in every situation, by prayer and petition, with thanksgiving, present your requests to God. And the peace of God, which transcends all understanding, will guard your hearts and your minds in Christ Jesus.**"

His peace transcends all understanding.

And my God will meet all your

needs according to the riches of his

glory in Christ Jesus.

Philippians 4:19

Peace not easy to accomplish because a the drop of dime we need to defend our self. Why can't we always be the bigger person and just say what ever someone do to me, I will still love them. How much better will our relationships be?

Longsuffering
(long and patient endurance of offense)

Longsuffering produces patience. I thought I knew what longsuffering meant because I have had three major surgeries and the recuperation time was approximately three months for each one. Three months was a long time, and in my opinion, I had patiently endured until I was healed.

However, that was just preparing me for what was to come. I have been on medical leave for several years because while walking at work, my right foot slid in a puddle of water and I landed on my left knee. As a result, I fractured my patella (knee cap) and injured the cartilage on my left knee. The fall appeared to be a simple fracture and surgery was not necessary. However, the injury I sustained was far worse than a fractured patella because I developed nerve damage referred to as Reflex Sympathetic Dystrophy (RSD). RSD is a debilitating disease of the nervous system that causes chronic pain, it is progressive and there is no known cure. One of the most common treatments used for RSD is sympathetic nerve blocks.

A sympathetic nerve block is performed by injecting steroids in the spinal canal with a needle. A big needle! The sympathetic nerves run on the front surface of the spinal column and not in the spinal canal with the nerves that provide sensation and strength to the leg. It is used to block the nerve for up to 8 hours hoping that it will reset itself to normal (less sensitivity to touch, movement and temperature). Therefore, the nerve block involved injecting steroids around the sympathetic nerves in my lower back. Did I mention that I am awake and they only use a local anesthetic while performing the nerve block? Suffice to say these procedures are not pleasant. I had to have several pain blocks. My leg pain did not improve and the steroids used brought on an onset of new problems; numbness in left hand, numbness in left foot, muscle spasm in my entire body (especially spinal column), increased blood pressure, increased blood sugars and severe pain in my abdomen. To make a long story short, I currently can not sit, stand, type on a computer or walk for any significant period of time without extreme pain. Furthermore, I can not exercise to combat the most visual side effect from the steroids – weight gain! Ugh! I gained 32 pounds in one year.

Mental State – My Mind

The injury affected my social life immediately. I had never been one to allow many visitors in my home. However, I was a social butterfly and a lover of conversing with and meeting new people. I went to work, attended church, dinner parties, birthday parties, theatre, travelled and the gym regularly. My calendar was quite full the majority of the time. However, that changed after the accident. My phone barely rang. A few people called to check on me, but the majority of my days were long and lonely. I was not able to participate in many of the activities I used to because the pain and swelling of my legs increased with movement. Yes, I wrote legs. Because relying heavily on the use of my right leg caused it to hurt as well.

Because of the weight gain I was withdrawn and it was a mental battle to conjure up the courage to be seen in public because I no longer looked like myself and I could not fit any of the clothing I once wore. The monetary benefit I received from Worker's Compensation was a pittance (60 percent) of my salary. I could barely pay my monthly obligations and the thought of purchasing something new to wear was like a dream. All of that contributed to my depression, loneliness and isolation.

As each day passed, my financial pressures increased. I did all I could to encourage myself. However, in the midst of that rough period in life I learned what friendship meant. Now I have clarity and definitely know who my friends are, who my acquaintances are and who was pretending.

In a nut shell, my mental state was challenged every waking moment of every day! Therefore, it was imperative that I prayed to maintain my sanity.

Spiritual State - My Soul

✕I began to realize the journey was spiritual. I could no longer depend on tangible things to make me happy. Reading my Bible and praying is what I had to do to survive and that is what I did as explained in my book entitled, *"Pray Into His Presence."*

I was raised in a Baptist church and I have not always been a spiritual person. However, I have always believed in the Trinity: the Father, the Son and the Holy

Ghost. God has always been my visitor and comforter when I was discouraged or troubled and I am happy I knew the importance of having a relationship with Jesus Christ prior to my injury. I shudder to think what I would have done if I had not known Him before I needed Him. He was and is my only constant friend.

Since I have been injured I have had to relearn who I am and what my talents and gifts are. Actually, I had to see myself and who I am more clearly than ever before. I also had to see what God had put before me and learn how to become understanding of my limited abilities. I realized I could not keep the "woe is me" attitude and make it through. I knew God had created me to be something, but I did not know all about my hidden talents until I became incapable of doing and being what I had created me to be. Did you get that? Not what God had created me to be, but what I had created me to be.

During that period of longsuffering by being patient I discovered my strengths, weaknesses and greater faith. This resulted in realizing I had no reason to feel lonely or sad because I had more reasons to be thankful. God showed me Him and how He works within my life when I surrendered to His will for me.

As of this writing, my journey of longsuffering is not finished, however my interpretation of my situation has changed. I have endured injury, trouble, hardship, financial pressures and provocation for quite some time. However, I am patiently enduring which means I have learned the true meaning of longsuffering. I realize my current situation is not a hindrance but a benefit of learning about me, my unknown talents and God given gifts. For example, you are reading this book because I am now an author, one of the many hidden talents that were revealed. Even though I no longer can type 100 wpm as I had prior to injury, I can use speech recognition software and produce the same outcome. So, I no longer feel sorry for myself. I am an overcomer and I know it.

Today, I am convinced that I am right where God would have me to be and He is right here with me. I am being perfected and equipped for my future.

What trauma, illness or trials do you think were used to equip you with being patient?

Have you gone through something that catapulted you to your next level in Christ?

Since longsuffering develops patience, can you recall a time when you were tested beyond what you thought you could handle?

This reminds me of a portion of my life verse as mentioned in the first section entitled Love. Romans 5-3 reads, **"Not only so, but we also glory in our sufferings, because we know that suffering produces perseverance; perseverance, character; and character, hope."** I had to learn how to rejoice during my time of hardship so I could be repaired, prepared and strengthened for my future. Simply put, my life verse was not selected by me. It was selected for me by God. Do you have a life verse? If not, seek His face by praying for God's guidance before selecting a verse, then be patient and observe how your life will follow that path.

*Jesus is and has been my most
constant, reliable, loveable,
peaceful and truly dependable
friend in my life.*

Gentleness
(considerate or kindly in disposition; amiable and tender....)

When I was younger I saw a United Negro College television commercial that stated, "The mind is a terrible thing to waste", which referenced the importance of education. However, after interacting with some extremely educated people, I wonder if it is it possible one can be considered "over educated"? This thought brings to mind one person I know that I believe has the "over educated" condition per se.

I met Candy when we were introduced by a mutual friend when I was 15 years old. Candy and I seemed to have more in common than we had with our mutual friend so she and I naturally developed a bond that grew into a close friendship.

We remained as close as two sisters from our youth until adulthood. I did not attend college immediately after High School, but Candy did. Actually, she attended a prominent college in a different city so I occasionally went to visit her there on campus. After graduation, Candy moved back home, fell in love and married her husband. I

44

was present at Candy's wedding and became the Godmother of her first child (at least that is what I was told). I was unable to attend the formal service for the christening because I was out of the country, so I never saw or signed official paperwork. However, Candy told me I was the other Godmother and I believed her. Yes, the other Godmother. Candy had another friend, whom she had met while in college, that was also the Godmother of her child.

Candy always had to have more than the ordinary. She had achieved all that she aspired: graduated college with honors, a husband, a beautiful child, enrolled in a masters program, a great job, a gorgeous home and yet, she still was not a happy person. As I think back, she never appeared to be satisfied with anything. She always wanted more than what she had. I believe this behavior was cultivated more while she attended the prestigious college. While there she learned how to blend in with others that were more cultured and wealthier than her and her family. As refined as she wanted to be, more often than not, Candy's behavior betrayed her desire. When angered or annoyed she exhibited the craziest screaming tantrums I had ever seen. However, I am certain this behavior was never displayed in front of her sorority sisters.

Unfortunately, she had become a master of deception while attending college.

Nevertheless, I knew her before she developed her "better than everyone" demeanor so we remained in contact with one another even though adulthood led us in different directions. After several years of marriage Candy revealed that she was getting a divorce because of her husband's extramarital affair. Her financial status would not allow her to maintain the mortgage payment on the beautiful new house they had recently purchased in the suburbs unless I would consider moving in to help her and my godchild. I was delighted and began to send resumes to prominent corporations in her area. It did not take long before I realized how easy it was going to be for me to get a new job, an increase in salary and to live in the suburbs.

My employment search ended quickly once I was hired by one of the top law firms in the country. I was employed as a Word Processor which was a position that paid me well and I was proud of it. Everything was working out better than planned. So, I happily moved in with Candy.

The first two months everything was great. My pay was great, the job was rewarding, the neighborhood and house was nice and spending quality time with my god child was lots of fun. At work I met new friends and enrolled in night classes. I was extremely busy and happy. Candy had a new boyfriend named, Martin, so we did not see each other often but we did converse throughout the day to update one another on each other's schedule. At times, I helped her more by picking up my godchild from school, but we mainly conversed in passing.

Why do things seem to change when you are having fun? I do not know, but as if on cue, things changed. Candy realized that my salary was very close to the amount she was being paid (she had a degree and was in grad school, I did not) and decided to ask me to pay more money toward utilities. Then the next week she wanted more money for rent. Her reason for the increases was not because her bills were increasing but because her boyfriend Martin was increasing his roommates rent at his house. I really believe jealousy and greed was the true motivation behind the requested increases, however, I gave her the additional increased amount.

The next rent increase from Candy was discussed when she called me on a Friday afternoon while I was at work. I objected to the increase and asked Candy to hold the line because the Managing Partner of the law firm had walked in to converse with me. I should have placed the call on hold, but I did not. I laid the phone down, stood up and hid the phone behind me. While he was explaining his visit and announcing to me I was being promoted to another position, I could hear Candy screaming through the phone receiver on my desk. I was elated that my boss could not hear her voice through the receiver. When the Managing Partner walked out of the office, I was so excited about my new promotion that I attempted to calm Candy down and share the good news with her. Candy was screaming and cursing so loudly that she could not hear me. Exasperated, I gave up, hung up the phone and decided to move out that evening after work.

One thing I had learned the hard way was to never argue with anyone in their house. Therefore, after work I went to her house, packed my clothes, left her keys and left. I had recently paid her rent so I did not owe her anything and I never contacted her to request a refund. I let her keep it as long as I did not have to deal with her any longer. The prior months were considered good because I avoided confrontations by not complaining or objecting to anything Candy said or wanted. For example, I never mentioned how my heater less room was cold all night because she turned the heat off at night. Every night I was cold. Yet, she wanted me to pay more for the utilities. Nor did I mention how small my room was. It was actually an office. My bed was smaller than a normal twin size bed and I did not have a lock on the door, which meant no privacy. However, I never complained that anyone could and did enter my room whenever they wanted to. There were so many things that I could have complained about but I knew I was better off moving back into my parent's home. Candy and I did not have contact with one another after I moved but I did hear she sold her house and moved to another state six months later.

28 or 29 years later while shopping I saw one of Candy's high school classmates who recalled I was also a friend of Candy's. Mickey told me she recently reunited with Candy and Candy's daughter, Ellen, was moving to Massachusetts to attend grad school. Even though Candy and I had not resolved the issues of the past, I was excited to hear of their impending visit. Actually, the problems of

the past no longer mattered to me. I always wondered how many children Candy had, where they were, if I was considered the worse godmother on earth and if my godchild was coming for a visit as well. I also wanted to see her and pictures of her life.

With my permission, Mickey gave Candy my phone number and Candy contacted me immediately. When Candy came to town, we met and conversed like old times. We never mentioned what happened to our friendship when I lived in her house. We just picked up where we were and did not discuss the past. I met Candy's youngest daughter, Ellen, who was Martin's daughter. When I realized she was going to live in the same city, without her immediate family, I basically adopted Ellen as part of my family. I gave her keys to my home, invited her to attend outings and introduced her to the city. I even allowed her to dine with me on holidays. It did not take long to discover Ellen was a lot like Candy. However, she was more miserable than I ever recall her mother being.

The more I conversed with Candy, the more I realized it was a mistake reuniting with her. She wholeheartedly believed that her opinion was the only opinion that mattered. I believe in every relationship one person is more knowledgeable than the other on different topics. Candy spoke as if she was the strongest, smartest or most refined of the two of us all the time. The truth of the matter is, I did not want to argue over nonsense and I was not going to debate with her on insignificant issues. Every topic we discussed there was a conflict of opinion so I attempted to find a neutral subject. She said she was a Christian so I tried to discuss Bible scriptures with her. However, we could not converse about the Bible and agree. Even though Candy did not read it much, she constantly suggested I changed my opinion of scripture interpretations and that I did not understand what was written. You see, Candy is more educated than I and automatically assumed she knew more. I felt sorry for her because her assumptions revealed how out of touch she was with reality. While Candy was studying and learning from text books, I was living a life that taught me how to rely on God and not my own understanding. Everything she knew was from a text book or her own personal summations on life.

Candy's daughter and I began to converse frequently because her daughter was in need of maternal guidance. Candy was cold and secretive so they did not have the mother and daughter relationship they could have had. Her daughter did not understand why her mother kept so many important issues and conversations hidden from her. I think it is because she knew her daughter's lack of discretion. Her daughter disclosed things to me about Candy that Candy had not shared with me.

As I listened to Ellen, I learned that I had been tricked into moving into Candy's house when we were younger. She was the one that was unfaithful to her husband, not the other way around. I further discovered that Candy was also unfaithful to Martin, who was her second husband and then she was unfaithful to him with her third husband. The third husband Candy never told me about because he had the same last name as her second husband and she did not think I would ever find out. Furthermore, her oldest child was never told who I was because I was not the godparent. Candy had lied to me about everything. It became apparent to me that Candy was untrustworthy and had many secrets that she did not want exposed. What a mess! I believe she hid these facts from me because she wanted me to think highly of her.

I wished she had not lied to me. I thought about our entire friendship to determine which offense bothered me the most. I needed to decide if I could live with the deceit and remain her friend or not. The fact that she was not loyal to the men she married only caused concern for me because it indicated more than just a lack of loyalty. In my opinion, it also indicated a lack of integrity, bad character, poor judgment and a person that was extremely untrustworthy. However, I discerned there was no point in revealing to her that I knew the truth.

I remained cordial and polite when she phoned, however it was difficult conversing with her because she spoke as if everyone else was living a lie; everyone accept her that is. I knew she was still prone to having tantrums because I heard her have one when she broke up with a male friend (to old to call him a boyfriend). I felt stuck. I no longer wanted to have a friendship with her because she was manipulative, argumentative and untrustworthy. However, I knew she would want to debate or argue about my decision to disassociate and terminate all communication with her and, in my opinion, my decision was not debatable.

My attempt to slowly distance myself became very stressful. Whenever Candy phoned I would get a headache. I realized the amount of time I allowed her to converse with me about her pretentious past life and current dilemmas was time I could use constructively in other ways. I had to figure out a way to explain to Candy that I wanted to reduce the amount of time we conversed. Therefore, I explained to her that my Bible reading time was beginning to suffer because I spent an excessive amount of time on the telephone. That ruffled her feathers and she did not receive it well. She began leaving condescending messages on my phone such as, "call me when you find time and you are not, hmm…(unnecessary pause) reading." Her sarcasm was undeniably unwarranted therefore I eventually stopped answering her calls and did not respond to her messages. As predicted, Candy had one of her infamous tantrums. She repeatedly called my phone, used words not worthy of repeating, called me names, text my phone continuously, left many angry messages and even instructed her daughter to never speak to me again. It was a repeat of her behavior from years prior. All I thought of was Titus 3:2 **"to slander no one, to be peaceable and considerate, and to show true humility toward all men."** I refused to respond because I knew she was trying to provoke me into reacting so she could feel justified about her behavior.

In my opinion, Candy had become an overachiever fueled by her insecurities and immaturity and still had not learned how to gracefully accept criticism, handle disagreements or accept a difference of opinion maturely. Her learned knowledge taught her about situations and circumstances; however her life experiences had not developed character that cultivated positive outcomes.

By the time I verbalized my desire to end my friendship with Candy I wanted her and her daughter, Ellen to happily live their lives without me. However, once Candy and I no longer conversed, Ellen began to call me more frequently. I had often heard her speak in a disrespectful manner about and to her mother so I constantly encouraged her to change her attitude/tone when they conversed. I unsuccessfully attempted to help foster a better relationship between them from a distance. However, her behavior raised red flags with me. I thoroughly believe if a person is over the age of 21 and disrespectful toward their parents and teachers, then nine times out of ten, that person will be disrespectful to all authority figures. Therefore, I knew it was just a matter of time before Ellen was disrespectful towards me. Once again, time proved me right.

The first time I did not agree with Ellen and told her that she was creating a problem for herself and I did not take her side in the matter, she abruptly ended the conversation and never spoke to me again. She even lied and said she had lost the keys to my home when I requested she return them. She was aware that she was responsible to pay for the replacement security key. However, Ellen text "I lost your keys and if you are concerned, you should either change your locks or contact the authorities". I thought "hmm, this apple did not fall far from the tree, but she definitely had less class than her mother." I knew that anything I said or did was going to reflect more on their opinion of who God is than on me so I said nothing.

I had attempted to introduce both Candy and Ellen to the God that I know and serve. I shared my vehicle, home, food, scriptures, prayers and testimonies of what God had and does for me. However, I do not believe either of them completely understood that He would also do it for them. Regardless, I knew that my reaction toward them could not be anything less than firm, gentle and non confrontational. If I had defended myself, they were both waiting to say, "Oh and you are a Christian?" in an accusatory tone. I have been there and heard that before so I knew how to handle the situation this time. I ended my association with both of them by ending all forms of communication. Sometimes actions speak louder than words when dealing with attention seekers.

I was proud that I could represent God in a gentle manner. Gentleness is a quality shown in a person's character and it can not be expressed in a violent verbal or nonverbal manner. As a Christian my actions do not just represent me, they represent the Christ in me. I could have chosen to expose all that I knew about Candy and Ellen, however, that would have resulted in me being reactive and not centered on my own values and strengths. True gentleness comes forth in times we recognize our capacity to respond harshly and instead choose to be tender or when we can inflict harm and instead embrace lovingly.

Have you been in situations where you could have proved to other's how strong your character is, but chose to display a gentler spirit because it showed true inner strength fueled by the Holy Spirit? Can you recall consciously thinking that your actions represent Christ in the midst of adversity? Can God trust you to demonstrate strength in the midst of adversity?

Proverbs 5:1 reads "**A gentle answer turns away wrath, but a harsh word stirs up anger.**" I had more than enough reasons to verbalize what Candy's actions stirred up inside of me, however, it would have only stirred up more dissension and arguing. If you want to settle a matter, use gentle words. 2 Timothy 2:24 reads "**And the Lord's servant must not be quarrelsome but must be kind to everyone, able to teach, not resentful.**" If you are a Christian your response to others should always be as a representative of Christ. Do not worry about how you appear to others. Your outward appearance is not as important as your inner peace. **Your beauty should not come from outward adornment, such as elaborate hairstyles and the wearing of gold jewelry or fine clothes. [4] Rather, it should be that of your inner self, the unfading beauty of a gentle and quiet spirit, which is of great worth in God's sight**" as in 1 Peter 3:3-4.

Delivering a harsh word is easy because we live in a society which is full of evil. But, choose to be different and more Christ like by seeking to develop and maintain a gentle spirit.

Be kind and compassionate to one another, forgiving each other, just as in Christ God forgave you.

Colossians 3:2

Goodness
(moral excellence, virtue)

Goodness. This is a word that I never thought much about until I closely evaluated my friendship with Susie.

. I met Susie a few years ago while volunteering two days a week at a youth program. Susie's daughter revealed to another volunteer leader that her mother was extremely abusive. She told the leader that her mother punched her in the face and beat her frequently since she was two years old. When I met Susie's daughter she was 12 years of age. The leader that she reported her abuse to only told me and did not report it to the overseers of the program. I conversed with Susie's daughter and attempted to get her to go with me and report it to people who could help her. Her daughter was adamant that she would not go to the authorities or reveal this information to the leaders of the youth program. I could not report this without substantiated evidence. Therefore, I ensured her that I would befriend Susie, so I could report her if I witnessed any abusive behavior.

Susie's daughter and I agreed to the plan and I introduced myself to her mother. As if timing could not have been better, her mother was having difficulty getting her deposit refunded after changing her mind about purchasing a home in the middle of the real estate transaction. I was employed as a real estate agent therefore, once she heard where I worked, she wanted to know what I knew. We exchanged phone numbers and began what I would call, a one sided relationship.

Susie told me about her dilemma. I listened and advised Susie of her rights and the steps required to have the real estate agency refund her money. Susie followed my advice and her money was immediately refunded. Her refund was a substantial amount of the selling price of the home. Therefore, I know she was extremely happy to have her money returned.

I occasionally dined with Susie and her daughter and since Susie was interested in purchasing a home, I began to send her listings for houses according to her desired specifications. However, I never heard from Susie regarding the listings or her desire to view homes, even though I attempted to contact her and follow up. Instead,

Susie purchased a home from another real estate agent and paid cash. Yes, she paid cash for the home. That would have been a great commission for me, but Susie only wanted my help when it was free - not my services as a professional real estate buyer's agent. Unfortunately, Susie purchased a house that is poorly constructed and has numerous problems. She had to install a gas heating system within the first year of its purchase. I know I would have advised her against purchasing that particular house. After I discovered she hired someone else to purchase her home, to protect my feelings of being overlooked, I had to remind myself the only reason I was friendly with her was for her daughter's benefit.

Over the past several years Susie professed to me that I was her closest friend. However, her treatment of me was less than what one would consider friendly. During this period of time I observed improved communications between her and her daughter which made my communication with Susie rewarding. I personally never witnessed any physical abuse however I did believe Susie was capable. It finally became apparent there was suspected abuse when her daughter's school reported their suspicions to the authorities. Susie quickly learned that she could be imprisoned if she was abusing her daughter. I believe that was the final time her daughter had to worry about being physically assaulted by her.

Once the issue of abuse was resolved, I continued to associate with Susie. Over time I observed behavior and heard conversations that revealed the true content of her heart. All of her thoughts and actions were controlled by money and her love for it. You see Susie is a millionaire but she is very cheap. Not frugal – cheap! Unfortunately for her, she gained her wealth because of tragedies in her life and did not have to work to acquire it.

She was rarely complimentary of others and their material possessions. I recall her words the first time she came to my home to visit. She said "This is it?" with her face frowned as if something was very smelly and unsatisfactory. Apparently she assumed my décor would and should have been more extravagant than it was. I ignored her because I could not afford to live like a millionaire. However, after her initial reaction, I decided to restrict her visits to my home. On one occasion she showed up uninvited and called to say she was outside. I went outside to converse with her but I did not invite her in.

Because she had very few friends and always expressed her desire to be invited to social events, I occasionally invited her to events I hosted. I soon discovered why she did not receive invitations often. When I invited her to a graduation party I thought it odd that she did not arrive with a gift, card or congratulatory word from her lips. I do not believe one should invite someone solely to receive a gift; however gifts are customary depending upon the occasion. I then invited Susie to my birthday party and she arrived without a card, gift or verbal "happy birthday", however she did ask me to purchase her an alcoholic beverage because she did not bring any money. Who does that? I had over 100 people present and no one else had the nerve to ask that of me.

After that I probably should not have invited Susie to a surprise party at a restaurant, but I did. I informed her that I ordered and prepaid for the food and everyone was responsible for ordering and paying for their own alcoholic beverage in advance. Every person that attended was aware of this arrangement and most of them purchased drinks as a birthday gift for the birthday person. However, when our waitress arrived, I observed Susie order a separate dish, without my permission and she stated it was only for her. I had to intervene when the food arrived and ensure it was shared with the other guests because it was charged to my bill. Furthermore, at this event, Susie stated that she purchased a beer from the bar as a birthday gift for the birthday person. However, when I received the bill, the beer she "purchased" was listed because she did not pay for it. She ordered it and allowed the bartender to include it on my tab with the expenses for the entire party

After observing her behavior, I realized that no matter what the circumstance or situation, if Susie could find a way to pay the least amount or nothing, she would. I was not comfortable discussing what I observed, so I did not mention it to her. I continued to converse with her but no longer invited her to social events. I had loss sight of why I befriended her in the first place. I had allowed her to insult me as a real estate agent, insult my home with comments upon her first visit and continuously vex my spirit with her mean spirited derogatory comments about others.

The final straw was when I learned she had deceived a food pantry and enrolled to receive free food. The food pantry's purpose is to aid less fortunate individuals and families by assisting them with food donations. Susie is so cheap that she does not mind being deceptive and standing in line to receive bags of food for herself. She told me that when she received food, she inspected her bags to separate what she wanted to keep and then gave away the remaining food items to other people that had no knowledge of her membership with the food pantry. She then deceived those people by allowing them to believe that she purchased the food solely to help them. She also collects turkeys at Thanksgiving time that are intended for families in need. Susie has so much food that her refrigerator and stand alone freezer are always filled to capacity. She can not store the food she receives from the food pantry so she has to ask others to allow her to store her food in their freezer. This was so upsetting for me that I stopped communicating with her entirely.

In my opinion, a person who does this has the same spirit as Ananias and Sapphira in the Bible. This is the story as recounted in Acts 5:1-11 (NIV): **Now a man named Ananias, together with his wife Sapphira, also sold a piece of property. With his wife's full knowledge he kept back part of the money for himself, but brought the rest and put it at the apostles' feet. Then Peter said,**

"Ananias, how is it that Satan has so filled your heart that you have lied to the Holy Spirit and have kept for yourself some of the money you received for the land? Did not it belong to you before it was sold? And after it was sold, wasn't the money at your disposal? What made you think of doing such a thing? You have not lied just to human beings but to God." When Ananias heard this, he fell down and died. And great fear seized all who heard what had happened. Then some young men came forward, wrapped up his body, and carried him out and buried him. About three hours later his wife came in, not knowing what had happened. Peter asked her, "Tell me, is this the price you and Ananias got for the land?" "Yes," she said, "that is the price." Peter said to her, "How could you conspire to test the Spirit of the Lord? Listen! The feet of the men who buried your husband are at the door, and they will carry you out also." At that moment she fell down at his feet and died. Then the young men came in and, finding her dead, carried her out and buried her beside her husband. Great fear seized the whole church and all who heard about these events."

This story of Ananias and Sapphira reminds me of Susie because they were wealthy, untruthful, had hardened hearts, were deceptive, cheap and lied to appear generous. They kept what they wanted and gave as if they were giving from the goodness of their heart. Until this encounter I always thought giving was motivated by love. I learned what goodness really means after I met someone who does not have generosity or excellence of character in her heart.

Suffice to say, I am no longer corresponding with Susie. Her daughter is an adult with her own child and living a productive life. So my mission was accomplished and Susie played an important role in teaching me about goodness. I realize I had to see the complete opposite of goodness to discover what it really means. Evilness is the opposite of goodness. Hmm, makes one think, doesn't it?

Have you encountered someone that is an enigma because he/she appears one way and yet when you observe him/her closely or listen to him/her speak, the person is completely different from what he/she appeared? Goodness in a person should reflect a character worthy of repeating and judgment of actions worthy of compliments.

The Good News (Bible) has many stories of goodness – Jesus fed the hungry, He healed the sick, and restored sight to the blind just to name a few. Pick up your Bible and read about Jesus and his goodness. As you read, you will learn how to let your light shine so your goodness will glorify God. **"In the same way, let your light shine before others, that they may see your good deeds and glorify your Father in heaven."** which is found in Matthew 5:16.

Set your minds on things above, not on earthly things.

Colossians 3:2

Faith
(loyalty, belief and trust in God)

I interpret faith as having an unwavering belief in something unseen. Even though I can not see it, I have faith that there is a divine blessing connected to tithing. In Malachi 3:10 it reads "**Bring the whole tithe into the storehouse, that there may be food in my house. Test me in this,**" says the LORD Almighty, "**and see if I will not throw open the floodgates of heaven and pour out so much blessing that there will not be room enough to store it**." I truly believe that if I tithe I will not have to worry about my bills and how they will be paid. I know I will have debt and I am required to pay it, but I will not worry. No worry means no stress for me. Therefore, I tithe most of the time. I would be untruthful if I say that I have tithed all the time. There have been times wherein I spent money too quickly and did not calculate correctly and before I realized it, I had spent my tithe or a portion of it. However, when I receive money and write my check for my tithe first and then do whatever else I am going to do with my money, I am successful with tithing. Just because

I have had times I did not tithe, does not mean I do not believe there is a divine blessing attached.

Since I can remember my debts have outweighed my income. However, as long as I tithe, all my debts get paid with money left over for additional purchases.

I recall what happened a few years ago when I did not tithe from my monthly pay check. Most months I would pay all of my tithe and monthly bills as soon as I received my check. However, this particular month, for some reason, that I do not recall now, I did not tithe and I spent the entire check on either bills or myself.

As the month progressed I realized I did not have enough food in the house to last until my next pay check. I immediately knew why. It was because I had not tithed. I decided I was not going to borrow money for food because I could stretch what I had and I also knew it was my fault. Furthermore, I knew it was not fair to ask someone to help me when I caused the problem. All I had to do was tithe.

What I failed to realize was my son was watching and noticed we did not have enough food in the house for the both of us. I had simply decided to eat less to ensure he had enough food.

I only had 3 more days until my pay day and we only had enough food in the house to prepare breakfast for my son before he left for school that day. I called my son and told him to eat breakfast and his response was "No Mom, you have not been eating and I can find a way to get something to eat at school". My son's school served free breakfast, but he was not on the government assisted free meal plan. I paid for his meals monthly. There was a $0 balance on his card and I did not have money to replenish it. Still, there was no way I was going to allow him to go to school and beg for food. I insisted that he ate the breakfast I had prepared and gave him all I had to pay for his lunch. I was saddened because my disobedience had not only created a problem for me, but it was also affecting my son. I knew I had to do something to change our predicament and I had to do it quickly.

I had a meeting scheduled that I could not cancel but I did not have enough gas to get to my meeting and back home. So not only did I need money for food, I needed gas and money for my son's lunch for 3 more days.

As I drove to the meeting I prayed and asked God for $100. I remember saying, "God please let me find a place to take my bracelet and pawn it for $100? That is all I will need for food and gas until Friday. Then on Friday when I get paid I could afford to pick it up from the pawn shop."

I knew I had to ask God about pawning the bracelet because I prayed about purchasing the bracelet before I purchased it. I used my first commission check when I was a real estate agent to make the purchase. I had originally purchased another bracelet, realized I had not prayed about spending the money and returned it to the store. I then prayed that God would lead me to a bracelet I could afford to purchase. When I found and purchased the next bracelet it was on sale for 65% less than the normal sale price yet it appraised for its total value. I knew it was the right purchase and I believed it was a gift from God.

My meeting was at a church. After arriving at the church and waiting for the person I was scheduled to meet, I was informed that she was sick and was not going to be able to meet with me. I thought "This is perfect. I will go into the sanctuary and pray before I try to find a pawn shop to get the $100 I need."

I walked into the sanctuary and noticed a woman sitting in the back conversing on her cell phone. I was not focused on her so instead of wondering why she was in the sanctuary using her cell phone I found a seat further up front so I could pray. As I sat down I overheard her talking and realized she was praying with someone that was in the hospital. I was touched and when she finished praying on her cell phone I turned around and asked her if she would pray with me. I had never asked someone I knew or did not know to pray with me but, I was happy she said "yes". I replied "Stay there I will come to you." I gathered my belongings and walked to the back of the sanctuary where she was sitting.

As I sat down, I placed my belongings on the chair to my right, turned toward her on my left and introduced myself. She told me her name and we held hands to begin to pray. Before either of us said another word, she dropped my hands, turned to her left, reached in her purse, took out an envelope, extended her hand with the envelope toward me and said, "This is your money. God told me to give it to you." I unconsciously balled up my hands and put them in my lap and said "What are you talking about?" She opened the envelope and showed me five $20 bills and then put the envelope on my lap and said "The last time I did not give the money God told me to give, I lost all of it. So if you do not want it, leave it in the chair. But, I can not take it back. It is yours. Furthermore, the Lord said if you ever sell your bracelet you are to get top dollar for it. That was my gift to you."

I could not believe what I was hearing or seeing. I immediately realized God had answered my prayer. He gave me the $100 I had just prayed for and confirmed it with a message regarding my bracelet. He also confirmed that it was a gift from Him. I cried in disbelief. Actually, I do not recall hearing her prayer. I praised, prayed, cried and thanked God more than ever. When I left she gave me her phone number, but when I called the number it was a disconnected number. I thought I was going to be able to repay her but I have never seen her again and have no way to locate her. She was not a member of the church I met her in. She said she stopped there that day to pray.

That is the day I learned the true meaning of faith. At that moment, I fully understood Romans 3:5 which reads, **"But if our unrighteousness brings out God's righteousness more clearly, what shall we say? That**

God is unjust in bringing his wrath on us? (I am using a human argument.)". This means that God is faithful even when we are not! Faith is not only about me and my thoughts. Faith is what God's spirit is. He is faithful. Of course, He desires for us to behave in a manner that is respectful and honorable, however, even if we fall short, He is going to do whatever He said He would do. Just believe in Him and His word.

Do you have faith? Do you know how your faith has been cultivated? Do you have a testimony you can give others to help them understand your reason for having faith? Do you realize how faithful God is?

Romans 3:12 reads, **"For by the grace given me I say to every one of you: Do not think of yourself more highly than you ought, but rather think of yourself with sober judgment, in accordance with the faith God has distributed to each of you."** I believe this scripture explains that our trials, triumphs and tribulations are what God uses to distribute as a tool to grow our faith. So, instead of thinking we are in control of situations we should turn them over to the creator of all things because God's faithfulness can not be measured. I am convinced our faith is strengthened by each trial we encounter and conquer.

Yet you desired faithfulness even in the womb;
you taught me wisdom in that secret place.

Psalm 51:6

Meekness
(characterized by patience and longsuffering, moderate, humble...)

I believe this chapter is going to be more appealing and revealing to women than men. Simply put, I am a woman and can relate to women and their thought pattern more than I can to men. I am not implying men should not read this. I am simply stating that I may sound biased, because I am writing from my viewpoint as a woman on how I believe men think.

A number of years ago I was contacted by someone who knew me when I was a teenager. He stated that he had a crush on me in high school but never got up the nerve to approach me. As a matter of fact, we had never spoken to one another until he saw me at a friend's birthday party. He then searched a social networking site until he located me to keep in contact.

The more we conversed the more comfortable I became and I began to wish he had approached me when we were younger. I believe we would have dated. I knew of him and his name but I did not know him personally because we were never introduced.

I was very impressed that he took the time to find me after seeing him at the party. We conversed daily and I learned that he was seriously ill and had been for two years. But overall, he was a good hard working, God fearing man that had a few set backs over the years.

I began to pray for his healing and researched natural solutions for the aches and pains he complained about. I located medications and gave them to him. I followed up with him to verify they were helping him recover.

When I first saw him at the party, he appeared gaunt and very thin. However, after he began taking the all natural medication and vitamins I gave to him, he began to improve and gain weight. After two months, he looked remarkably different. If I were not keeping his identity private, I would show his pictures in this book. He looked like an entirely different person and extremely handsome!

As I stated earlier, he had some setbacks and unfortunately he became unemployed again before he was completely healed. It seems to me that men loose their identity when their income is reduced or they are not gainfully employed. However, he was determined to seek additional employment and pay his bills as best he could. Whenever the Lord put it on my heart, I would help him pay a few bills or to get food. I noticed whenever I was obedient and gave whatever the Lord directed me to give the money would come back to me from another source. In essence, I did not give anything that was not given back to me. Luke 6:38 reads, **"Give, and it will be given to you. A good measure, pressed down, shaken together and running over, will be poured into your lap. For with the measure you use, it will be measured to you."** Which means whatever you give, it will be given back to you. This further strengthened my belief that after I tithe, there is a divine financial covering connected to all of my finances which includes what I give to others because each time the same amount of money was returned to me.

The more I helped, the more distant he became. I have heard that a man is not comfortable with himself when he can not provide at a level that he has determined is acceptable. However, I thought he would have been thankful because some of his problems were getting solved, but he seemed to become resentful. Yes, he changed and I was puzzled. I do not know if it was because he was not happy with himself or because God kept replenishing my finances and not his. Regardless, I began to notice that he never said "thank you" anymore. He seemed not to care if he received help or not. When we conversed, his topics were negative and sad even though his circumstance was gradually improving. He was definitely going through a difficult period, but that was an excuse because gratitude is not limited to when our life is great.

One day he called and asked if he could borrow money from me. I know that he must have felt horrible having to ask to borrow from me. However, his timing was not good. I did not have any money I could loan him. Once I answered no, he became irate and insulting. I was infuriated. I had helped this person in the past and now that he was not getting what he wanted, when he wanted it, he insulted me and acted like a spoiled brat. I did not like it and after that day stopped communicating with him. However, the Lord would occasionally put it on my heart to send him assistance. Yes, I sent help even though we were not communicating. I sent it because God put it on my heart to send it. This was contrary to how I felt about our friendship and his behavior. But, I knew this was not about me. I was still on assignment and it was about the God I serve.

A few months passed before he contacted me. I suspected he would not apologize and I was correct, he did not. Nor did he say thank you for my assistance rendered when we were not in contact with one another. He conversed as if nothing had happened and as if there was no gap in our communication. I forgive very easily because I would rather have peace than dissension. But, I said nothing because I knew that I did not have to remind him of something he did that was offensive because in this case, he already knew.

He never asked to borrow money again. Funny thing, I was never directed to give him any more after that either. I believe meekness was being cultivated in me and I was showing strength even though it was perceived as weakness. Instead of being boisterous and argumentative because I was the one rendering the help and had been offended, I had to be quiet and continue to help during our season of adversity. I had to be humble and realize it was not about me.

I believe some men think single women who are nice, helpful and Godly are desperate. They do not understand that some single Godly women are not helpful solely because they are trying to impress him or because he needs help, but perhaps because she knows far more than he thinks. She is representing the God she serves, not the man. In this case, it is unfortunate that my friend did not realize God was the one getting the glory. I knew I was doing things that had not previously been in my character and I also knew that God was the reason. God had used strangers to help me in the past and I knew I was on assignment to help my friend. I never discussed this with him because I saw the meekness developing within myself and was hopeful that God was pleased. I felt pain once I realized we were not the friends I thought but again, instead of striking back, I harbored no resentment. We have remained friendly, but the friendship is not the same.

I can not say it loud enough that it is important you are very clear why you are helping someone. There are times we help people for the wrong reason. Sometimes it is to earn their friendship, attention, love, or to gain power over them and in some cases trap a husband/wife. Having a hidden agenda can cause you to get hurt because you may seek something that the person is unable to give. Unfortunately, people that are in need may entice you with whatever is needed to get what they want. Always be mindful when you help others and check your motive first. If you do, you will be able to remain meek and mild mannered if the person is irate, unthankful and rude after you have given assistance because your true intention was to render help and let God do the rest.

Have you ever been misunderstood by a man/woman who perceived your kindness as desperation? Have you learned to check your motive and agenda before helping someone?

Some women pretend to be kind and helpful (does not know the value of receiving the care and love she deserves from a man) just so she can be viewed as having characteristics similar to the Proverbs 31 woman. Proverbs 31:10-31 reads "**Wife of noble character who can find? She is worth far more than rubies. Her husband has full confidence in her and lacks nothing of value. She brings him good, not harm, all the days of her life. She selects wool and flax and works with eager hands. She is like the merchant ships, bringing her food from afar.**

She gets up while it is still night; she provides food for her family and portions for her female servants. She considers a field and buys it; out of her earnings she plants a vineyard. She sets about her work vigorously; her arms are strong for her tasks. She sees that her trading is profitable, and her lamp does not go out at night. In her hand she holds the distaff and grasps the spindle with her fingers. She opens her arms to the poor and extends her hands to the needy. When it snows, she has no fear for her household; for all of them are clothed in scarlet. She makes coverings for her bed; she is clothed in fine linen and purple. Her husband is respected at the city gate, where he takes his seat among the elders of the land. She makes linen garments and sells them, and supplies the merchants with sashes. She is clothed with strength and dignity; she can laugh at the days to come. She speaks with wisdom, and faithful instruction is on her tongue. She watches over the affairs of her household and does not eat the bread of idleness. Her children rise and call her blessed; her husband also, and he praises her: "Many women do noble things, but you surpass them all." Charm is deceptive, and beauty is fleeting; but a woman who fears the LORD is to be praised. Honor her for all that

her hands have done, and let her works bring her praise at the city gate.

Wow what a woman. In our limited understanding, she is depicted as a noble woman and the perfect wife (or potential wife). As a godly woman who fears the Lord and takes exceptional care of her family by being strong and dedicated. However, I believe these scriptures do not refer to a woman at all as referenced in The Passion Translation of the Bible. Yet, all women have the capability of being noble (having or showing fine personal qualities, high moral principles). Unfortunately, out of impatience of being single, some women may try to put the cart before the horse by pretending to possess the characteristics of a noble woman before surrendering herself to God. Nothing good will come from pretending. If the man does not love you for who God has made you to be, then he is not for you. Remember to be patient and honest for the best outcome.

Women, I have heard that men determine who we are and how far they think they would like to go with us relationship wise, when they first meet us. Unfortunately, some men are looking for a woman to step into the wife role without truly wanting her to be his wife. While other men, thinking you are a possible candidate, will watch you and judge you according to how he wants his wife to be (even though you are not his wife yet). This is very confusing for us women and not fair that we are judged prior to the title. That is like having a performance review prior to getting hired for the job. So single ladies I suggest; if the man is not your husband and God has not made it clear that you are to help him in any way, then do not pretend to be meek and helpful to portray someone you are not to gain his heart. It does not matter how it appears being deceitful can destroy the entire relationship.

You have to be strong to be meek because meekness is often misinterpreted as weakness. Be patient and do not worry, if God is cultivating meekness in you, then humility is also being developed as well. Please be obedient. As meekness grows within your character, it will become apparent in your mannerisms. Rest assured God has a plan for the meek - He said it in His word.

Blessed are the meek,
for they will inherit the earth.
Matthew 5:5

Temperance
(habitual moderation in the indulgence of the appetites or passions)

Temperance is having self-control and/or patience. It took a long time for me to develop self-control. It appears God used Mary to teach me about temperance.

When Mary and I met we immediately became friends. We had a lot of fun going to parties, skipping classes, and most things that teenage girls did behind their parents back. We went to different high schools so there were times we met for breakfast instead of going directly to school. I thought Mary was a friend and never imagined she would ever do anything to harm me.

As long as I did what Mary wanted to do we were friends. However, I soon grew tired of cutting classes and not doing what I was suppose to and began attending classes, completing my homework and behaving like a 15 year old should. Mary still appeared to be my friend, but she was secretly getting a group of girls together to beat me up after school. I did not completely understand why she wanted to harm me for doing what I was suppose to, but when I heard of her plan, I prepared for their ambush. Instead of waiting for all of them to jump on me when we met after school, I grabbed Mary and her and I fought. Subsequently, I was suspended from school and Mary was in trouble for trespassing. After the fight, I transferred to a different school. Many years passed before we saw one another again.

As adults, we greeted one another when we attended the same functions. We probably saw each other once every 3 to 4 years. Over time it became easier to greet her and we eventually exchanged phone numbers. We began sending each other invitations to functions we were hosting and slowly became friends again.

I was giving her the benefit of the doubt and believed that the things that happened when we where younger were issues of the past. In hindsight, she appeared to be my friend so when she invited me to a "girl's night out group" that had formed, I decided to join.

I thought it was great to have contact with someone from high school that I could reminisce with about people, places and things that no longer existed. Mary and I had similar interests in movies, events and theatre plays. I was glad she understood that I did not judge her according to her past behavior. I happily attended functions and went on trips out of state with her and the "girl's night out group". It was fun until scheduling conflicts between everyone made it impossible to attend events. Spending quality time together I learned more about Mary's past hurts and hardships during the years we were not friendly toward one another. I began to feel sorry for her. I truly wished that Mary took a bigger interest in learning more about God to help her learn more about forgiveness. So I constantly invited her to church, however she would not attend. So, I prayed for her and kept most of my thoughts/comments to myself.

Before the group dismantled, during one of our monthly "girl's night out" events, Mary informed me that a man was enquiring about me. From her description I thought I knew who the man was and asked her if she knew his name or anything about him, Mary replied "No" to both of my questions. I replied "I think you are referring to the guy who is stalking me and I hope you did not tell him anything about me". Mary looked at me with an arrogant and annoyed look and said, "Well I did tell him about you and your new work schedule." I was shocked that she would tell a stranger anything about me. The fact that she was confrontational when she responded to my question made me realize she was meaner than what she was when we were attending high school. I had to use all the self-control I could gather to keep from telling her everything I thought at that moment.

I was informed by someone else that her meeting with the mystery man happened a few days prior to our "girl's night out" meeting. Apparently, as Mary exited a department store a man approached her and asked her if she knew Vikki Harris. Mary responded "Yes". He stated that he "Thought he had seen her with me and he had not seen me in a while and was wondering how and where I was." Even though she did not know him or recall ever seeing him she proceeded to tell him about me and my new work schedule. A true friend would have taken his number and said "I will give her your information."

From that day forward when I conversed with Mary I did not share any of my personal information. I only shared biblical stories and scriptures. I also limited the number of functions I attended with her present. The other women from the group could not understand why I did not confront Mary and express my dislike of her blatant disregard for me and my safety. I did not say anything because I cared more about what God thought than what Mary thought. I also believed that I could never get her to believe in God if I behaved like her or worse. Besides I knew she did not care about anything other than her own thoughts and desires.

As time past I realized Mary was still the same sneaky Mary from high school. She began dating a married man that I asked her not to date. There are the obvious reasons why she should not have dated him, but also because his wife was someone that I knew fairly well. I noticed her flirting with him and I hoped that she had taken my advice. I later found out that she was dating him and did not want me to know. I was disappointed in this for so many reasons, but mainly because she did not value herself more.

Wisdom kept me from exposing what I knew. I watched her betray our friendship on numerous occasions. Her constant callous disregard for me as a human being and responding to me rudely whenever I attempted to discuss incidents with her was, at times, more difficult than what it should have been.

I had made a conscious decision to use self-control and patience whenever I conversed with her. It was difficult because Mary did not realize I knew she was not a truthful person. Sometimes when people do not realize their true agenda and phony character has been exposed, they will not try to behave better....they think they have mastered the deception and behave worse. At least that is what Mary did.

It took three years before I was convinced the problem was that Mary and I had not resolved our past issues and the reason we could not go forward was because the same resentment she had for me in high school was still there. There were only two things I was certain of; I still could not trust her and she was still very deceitful. I guess we were never really friends. Have you had friendships that never made sense? Have you considered someone your friend that did not consider you theirs?

When I read Proverbs 25:28, **"Like a city whose walls are broken through is a person who lacks self-**

control." I thought about my experience with Mary. If I had not been patient, used self control and handled the relationship with care, I would have been the Christian not standing on a firm foundation which represents Jesus Christ. I would have been like that city whose walls were broken. I had to make adjustments and not spend much time with Mary, but I did not have to compromise my walk with Christ while doing so. When one learns to use self-control and patience in a matter, wisdom is revealed. I used to pray for wisdom because James 1:5 reads "**If any of you lacks wisdom, you should ask God, who gives generously to all without fault, and it will be given to you.**" I asked God for wisdom and reflecting on my friendship with Mary, I saw that my request had been granted.

My reward for using self control when conversing with Mary was peace. I am at peace with myself because I learned how to discern Mary's spirit and not confront or converse with her in an adversary manner, but distance myself from her in a loving way.

For I know the plans I have for you, declares the LORD, plans to prosper you and not to harm you, plans to give you hope and a future.

Jeremiah 29:11

Most of us have had experiences wherein we were hurt by the absence of love, hateful words, jealousy, betrayal, unfaithfulness and/or deceitful people. None of those are attributes of God. As I reflected on each fruit (circumstance), I know I did not make a conscious decision to handle all the situations correctly. Most often, I made the right decision because I was hurt and did not know what to do, so I did nothing.

In hindsight, I believe these particular experiences are highlighted in my mind because they represent when my behavior was different than normal. I do not recall other life lessons I could have illustrated wherein I did not respond and make the situation worse. Some of these experiences were teachable moments for me wherein I thought to myself "I will not do that again" or "thank you God."

Each individual fruit is used to equip us for service in God's kingdom and knowing that God's ways are higher and more complex than what our minds can conceive, we no longer need to become excited or exasperated if confronted with negativity. Take comfort in knowing, it is okay to trust the process even when we cannot trust the personalities of people. Therefore, in conclusion, I realize that each person and his/her impact on my life have made me a better person and I am thankful that God allowed me to experience every encounter. I pray that God has or will show you the fruit of the spirit as it relates to you in a recognizable way.

Quick Reference Guide

As a quick reference, these scriptures can provide further insight into the biblical meaning of each fruit. It is suggested that the scriptures are read in its entirety by reading previous and preceding scriptures to receive insight into its interpretation.

Love

Psalm 63:3
Exodus 15:13
Leviticus 19:18
Deuteronomy 6:4-6
Deuteronomy 7:9

Longsuffering

2 Peter 3:9
Romans 8:28
Ephesians 4:2
Romans 2:4
2 Peter 3:9

Joy

Deuteronomy 16:15
Nehemiah 8:10
Esther 8:17
Ecclesiastes 9:7
Isaiah 9:3

Gentleness

Proverbs 15:1
Philippians 4:5
1 Peter 3:15
Titus 3:2
James 3:17

Peace

Proverbs 20:3
John 14:27
John 16:33
Romans 14:17
Philippians 4:7

Goodness

Romans 8:28
Psalm 23:6
Psalm 31:19
Psalm 65:4
James 3:13

Faith

Philippians 4:13
2 Corinthians 5:7
Ephesians 2:8
Mark 9:23
Matthew 9:22

Temperance

Titus 2:12
1 Corinthians 9:27
Romans 13:14
1 Peter 5:8
Proverbs 25:16

Meekness

Psalm 25:9
Matthew 11:29
1 Thessalonians 2:7
1 Thessalonians 5:15
Philippians 2:15

Made in the USA
Charleston, SC
08 March 2014